*This Journal Belongs To*

_____

# USING THIS JOURNAL/ PLANNER

Space to note down all appointments

| # WEEK | APPOINTMENTS | |
|---|---|---|
| 🗓 DATE | | : |
| 🕐 TIME | | : |
| 📍 PLACE | | : |

Space to note down daily/weekly goals and check-off on completion

| 💬 COMMUNICATION GOALS | |
|---|---|
| ☐ | ☐ |
| ☐ | ☐ |
| ☐ | ☐ |

| 👥 SOCIAL SKILLS GOALS | |
|---|---|
| ☐ | ☐ |
| ☐ | ☐ |
| ☐ | ☐ |

| ⚙ SENSORY & O.T. GOALS | |
|---|---|
| ☐ | ☐ |
| ☐ | ☐ |
| ☐ | ☐ |

Use space to note down therapy activity ideas

| 🧩 THERAPY ACTIVITY IDEAS | |
|---|---|
| VISUAL | AUDITORY |
| . | . |
| . | . |
| FINE MOTOR | TACTILE |
| . | . |
| . | . |

**Hope this journal helps. Take care and all the best!**

Please remember – Autism planner is only an aid to help you plan for the learning goal and achievements. It is in no ways a professional advice. All goals and their importance should be planned only in consultation with your special educator/ therapist

**SPECIAL REQUEST TO YOU**

If you like this journal and would like others to benefit from this – Your Amazon rating and review will help them take the buying decision.

Help us help them!

| # WEEK | | APPOINTMENTS | |
|---|---|---|---|
| ▦ DATE | | | : |
| 🕐 TIME | | | : |
| ◎ PLACE | | | : |

## 💬 COMMUNICATION GOALS

| ☐ | ☐ |
|---|---|
| ☐ | ☐ |
| ☐ | ☐ |

## 👥 SOCIAL SKILLS GOALS

| ☐ | ☐ |
|---|---|
| ☐ | ☐ |
| ☐ | ☐ |

## SENSORY & O.T. GOALS

| ☐ | ☐ |
|---|---|
| ☐ | ☐ |
| ☐ | ☐ |

## 🧩 THERAPY ACTIVITY IDEAS

| VISUAL | AUDITORY |
|---|---|
| • | • |
| • | • |
| **FINE MOTOR** | **TACTILE** |
| • | • |
| • | • |

| # WEEK | | APPOINTMENTS | |
|---|---|---|---|
| 🗓 DATE | | | : |
| 🕐 TIME | | | : |
| 📍 PLACE | | | : |

## 💬 COMMUNICATION GOALS

| ☐ | ☐ |
|---|---|
| ☐ | ☐ |
| ☐ | ☐ |

## 👥 SOCIAL SKILLS GOALS

| ☐ | ☐ |
|---|---|
| ☐ | ☐ |
| ☐ | ☐ |

## 🔲 SENSORY & O.T. GOALS

| ☐ | ☐ |
|---|---|
| ☐ | ☐ |
| ☐ | ☐ |

## 🧩 THERAPY ACTIVITY IDEAS

| VISUAL | AUDITORY |
|---|---|
| • | • |
| • | • |
| **FINE MOTOR** | **TACTILE** |
| • | • |
| • | • |

| # WEEK | | APPOINTMENTS | |
|---|---|---|---|
| ▦ DATE | | | : |
| ⏱ TIME | | | : |
| ⊚ PLACE | | | : |

## 💬 COMMUNICATION GOALS

| ☐ | ☐ |
|---|---|
| ☐ | ☐ |
| ☐ | ☐ |

## 👥 SOCIAL SKILLS GOALS

| ☐ | ☐ |
|---|---|
| ☐ | ☐ |
| ☐ | ☐ |

## ⚖ SENSORY & O.T. GOALS

| ☐ | ☐ |
|---|---|
| ☐ | ☐ |
| ☐ | ☐ |

## 🧩 THERAPY ACTIVITY IDEAS

| VISUAL | AUDITORY |
|---|---|
| • | • |
| • | • |

| FINE MOTOR | TACTILE |
|---|---|
| • | • |
| • | • |

| # WEEK | | APPOINTMENTS | |
|---|---|---|---|
| 📅 DATE | | | : |
| 🕐 TIME | | | : |
| 📍 PLACE | | | : |

## 💬 COMMUNICATION GOALS

| ☐ | ☐ |
|---|---|
| ☐ | ☐ |
| ☐ | ☐ |

## 👥 SOCIAL SKILLS GOALS

| ☐ | ☐ |
|---|---|
| ☐ | ☐ |
| ☐ | ☐ |

## SENSORY & O.T. GOALS

| ☐ | ☐ |
|---|---|
| ☐ | ☐ |
| ☐ | ☐ |

## 🧩 THERAPY ACTIVITY IDEAS

| VISUAL | AUDITORY |
|---|---|
| • | • |
| • | • |
| FINE MOTOR | TACTILE |
| • | • |
| • | • |

| # WEEK | APPOINTMENTS | |
|---|---|---|
| 🗓 DATE | | : |
| 🕐 TIME | | : |
| 📍 PLACE | | : |

## 💬 COMMUNICATION GOALS

| ☐ | ☐ |
|---|---|
| ☐ | ☐ |
| ☐ | ☐ |

## 👥 SOCIAL SKILLS GOALS

| ☐ | ☐ |
|---|---|
| ☐ | ☐ |
| ☐ | ☐ |

## SENSORY & O.T. GOALS

| ☐ | ☐ |
|---|---|
| ☐ | ☐ |
| ☐ | ☐ |

## 🧩 THERAPY ACTIVITY IDEAS

| VISUAL | AUDITORY |
|---|---|
| • | • |
| • | • |

| FINE MOTOR | TACTILE |
|---|---|
| • | • |
| • | • |

| # WEEK | | APPOINTMENTS | |
|---|---|---|---|
| 🗓 DATE | | | : |
| 🕐 TIME | | | : |
| 📍 PLACE | | | : |

## 💬 COMMUNICATION GOALS

| ☐ | ☐ |
|---|---|
| ☐ | ☐ |
| ☐ | ☐ |

## 👥 SOCIAL SKILLS GOALS

| ☐ | ☐ |
|---|---|
| ☐ | ☐ |
| ☐ | ☐ |

## 🔷 SENSORY & O.T. GOALS

| ☐ | ☐ |
|---|---|
| ☐ | ☐ |
| ☐ | ☐ |

## 🧩 THERAPY ACTIVITY IDEAS

| VISUAL | AUDITORY |
|---|---|
| • | • |
| • | • |
| FINE MOTOR | TACTILE |
| • | • |
| • | • |

| # WEEK | | APPOINTMENTS | |
|---|---|---|---|
| 📅 DATE | | | : |
| 🕐 TIME | | | : |
| 📍 PLACE | | | : |

## 💬 COMMUNICATION GOALS

| ☐ | ☐ |
|---|---|
| ☐ | ☐ |
| ☐ | ☐ |

## 👥 SOCIAL SKILLS GOALS

| ☐ | ☐ |
|---|---|
| ☐ | ☐ |
| ☐ | ☐ |

## 🔷 SENSORY & O.T. GOALS

| ☐ | ☐ |
|---|---|
| ☐ | ☐ |
| ☐ | ☐ |

## 🧩 THERAPY ACTIVITY IDEAS

| VISUAL | AUDITORY |
|---|---|
| • | • |
| • | • |

| FINE MOTOR | TACTILE |
|---|---|
| • | • |
| • | • |

| # WEEK | | APPOINTMENTS | |
|---|---|---|---|
| 🗓 DATE | | | : |
| 🕐 TIME | | | : |
| 📍 PLACE | | | : |

## 💬 COMMUNICATION GOALS

| ☐ | ☐ |
|---|---|
| ☐ | ☐ |
| ☐ | ☐ |

## 👥 SOCIAL SKILLS GOALS

| ☐ | ☐ |
|---|---|
| ☐ | ☐ |
| ☐ | ☐ |

## 🔷 SENSORY & O.T. GOALS

| ☐ | ☐ |
|---|---|
| ☐ | ☐ |
| ☐ | ☐ |

## 🧩 THERAPY ACTIVITY IDEAS

| VISUAL | AUDITORY |
|---|---|
| • | • |
| • | • |

| FINE MOTOR | TACTILE |
|---|---|
| • | • |
| • | • |

| # WEEK | | APPOINTMENTS | |
|---|---|---|---|
| 📅 DATE | | | : |
| 🕐 TIME | | | : |
| 📍 PLACE | | | : |

## 💬 COMMUNICATION GOALS

| ☐ | ☐ |
|---|---|
| ☐ | ☐ |
| ☐ | ☐ |

## 👥 SOCIAL SKILLS GOALS

| ☐ | ☐ |
|---|---|
| ☐ | ☐ |
| ☐ | ☐ |

## 🙌 SENSORY & O.T. GOALS

| ☐ | ☐ |
|---|---|
| ☐ | ☐ |
| ☐ | ☐ |

## 🧩 THERAPY ACTIVITY IDEAS

| VISUAL | AUDITORY |
|---|---|
| • | • |
| • | • |

| FINE MOTOR | TACTILE |
|---|---|
| • | • |
| • | • |

| # WEEK | APPOINTMENTS | |
|---|---|---|
| ▦ DATE | | : |
| 🕐 TIME | | : |
| ◎ PLACE | | : |

## 💬 COMMUNICATION GOALS

| ☐ | ☐ |
|---|---|
| ☐ | ☐ |
| ☐ | ☐ |

## 👥 SOCIAL SKILLS GOALS

| ☐ | ☐ |
|---|---|
| ☐ | ☐ |
| ☐ | ☐ |

## 🔲 SENSORY & O.T. GOALS

| ☐ | ☐ |
|---|---|
| ☐ | ☐ |
| ☐ | ☐ |

## 🧩 THERAPY ACTIVITY IDEAS

| VISUAL | AUDITORY |
|---|---|
| • | • |
| • | • |
| **FINE MOTOR** | **TACTILE** |
| • | • |
| • | • |

| # WEEK | APPOINTMENTS | |
|---|---|---|
| 📅 DATE | | : |
| 🕐 TIME | | : |
| 📍 PLACE | | : |

## 💬 COMMUNICATION GOALS

| ☐ | ☐ |
|---|---|
| ☐ | ☐ |
| ☐ | ☐ |

## 👥 SOCIAL SKILLS GOALS

| ☐ | ☐ |
|---|---|
| ☐ | ☐ |
| ☐ | ☐ |

## SENSORY & O.T. GOALS

| ☐ | ☐ |
|---|---|
| ☐ | ☐ |
| ☐ | ☐ |

## 🧩 THERAPY ACTIVITY IDEAS

| VISUAL | AUDITORY |
|---|---|
| • | • |
| • | • |

| FINE MOTOR | TACTILE |
|---|---|
| • | • |
| • | • |

| # WEEK | | APPOINTMENTS | |
|---|---|---|---|
| 📅 DATE | | | : |
| 🕐 TIME | | | : |
| 📍 PLACE | | | : |

## 💬 COMMUNICATION GOALS

| | | | |
|---|---|---|---|
| ☐ | | ☐ | |
| ☐ | | ☐ | |
| ☐ | | ☐ | |

## 👥 SOCIAL SKILLS GOALS

| | | | |
|---|---|---|---|
| ☐ | | ☐ | |
| ☐ | | ☐ | |
| ☐ | | ☐ | |

## 🔺 SENSORY & O.T. GOALS

| | | | |
|---|---|---|---|
| ☐ | | ☐ | |
| ☐ | | ☐ | |
| ☐ | | ☐ | |

## 🧩 THERAPY ACTIVITY IDEAS

| VISUAL | AUDITORY |
|---|---|
| • | • |
| • | • |
| **FINE MOTOR** | **TACTILE** |
| • | • |
| • | • |

| # WEEK | | APPOINTMENTS | |
|---|---|---|---|
| 📅 DATE | | | : |
| 🕐 TIME | | | : |
| 📍 PLACE | | | : |

## 💬 COMMUNICATION GOALS

| ☐ | ☐ |
|---|---|
| ☐ | ☐ |
| ☐ | ☐ |

## 👥 SOCIAL SKILLS GOALS

| ☐ | ☐ |
|---|---|
| ☐ | ☐ |
| ☐ | ☐ |

## 🧩 SENSORY & O.T. GOALS

| ☐ | ☐ |
|---|---|
| ☐ | ☐ |
| ☐ | ☐ |

## 🧩 THERAPY ACTIVITY IDEAS

| VISUAL | AUDITORY |
|---|---|
| • | • |
| • | • |
| FINE MOTOR | TACTILE |
| • | • |
| • | • |

| # WEEK | | APPOINTMENTS | |
|---|---|---|---|
| 📅 DATE | | | : |
| 🕐 TIME | | | : |
| 📍 PLACE | | | : |

## 💬 COMMUNICATION GOALS

| ☐ | ☐ |
|---|---|
| ☐ | ☐ |
| ☐ | ☐ |

## 👥 SOCIAL SKILLS GOALS

| ☐ | ☐ |
|---|---|
| ☐ | ☐ |
| ☐ | ☐ |

## 🧩 SENSORY & O.T. GOALS

| ☐ | ☐ |
|---|---|
| ☐ | ☐ |
| ☐ | ☐ |

## 🧩 THERAPY ACTIVITY IDEAS

| VISUAL | AUDITORY |
|---|---|
| • | • |
| • | • |
| FINE MOTOR | TACTILE |
| • | • |
| • | • |

| # WEEK | | APPOINTMENTS | |
|---|---|---|---|
| 📅 DATE | | | : |
| 🕐 TIME | | | : |
| 📍 PLACE | | | : |

## 💬 COMMUNICATION GOALS

| ☐ | ☐ |
|---|---|
| ☐ | ☐ |
| ☐ | ☐ |

## 👥 SOCIAL SKILLS GOALS

| ☐ | ☐ |
|---|---|
| ☐ | ☐ |
| ☐ | ☐ |

## 🔷 SENSORY & O.T. GOALS

| ☐ | ☐ |
|---|---|
| ☐ | ☐ |
| ☐ | ☐ |

## 🧩 THERAPY ACTIVITY IDEAS

| VISUAL | AUDITORY |
|---|---|
| • | • |
| • | • |

| FINE MOTOR | TACTILE |
|---|---|
| • | • |
| • | • |

| # WEEK | | APPOINTMENTS | |
|---|---|---|---|
| 🗓 DATE | | | : |
| 🕐 TIME | | | : |
| 📍 PLACE | | | : |

## 💬 COMMUNICATION GOALS

| ☐ | ☐ |
|---|---|
| ☐ | ☐ |
| ☐ | ☐ |

## 👥 SOCIAL SKILLS GOALS

| ☐ | ☐ |
|---|---|
| ☐ | ☐ |
| ☐ | ☐ |

## 🔶 SENSORY & O.T. GOALS

| ☐ | ☐ |
|---|---|
| ☐ | ☐ |
| ☐ | ☐ |

## 🧩 THERAPY ACTIVITY IDEAS

| VISUAL | AUDITORY |
|---|---|
| • | • |
| • | • |
| FINE MOTOR | TACTILE |
| • | • |
| • | • |

| # WEEK | | APPOINTMENTS | |
|---|---|---|---|
| ▦ DATE | | | : |
| ⏲ TIME | | | : |
| ⊚ PLACE | | | : |

## 💬 COMMUNICATION GOALS

| ☐ | ☐ |
|---|---|
| ☐ | ☐ |
| ☐ | ☐ |

## SOCIAL SKILLS GOALS

| ☐ | ☐ |
|---|---|
| ☐ | ☐ |
| ☐ | ☐ |

## SENSORY & O.T. GOALS

| ☐ | ☐ |
|---|---|
| ☐ | ☐ |
| ☐ | ☐ |

## 🧩 THERAPY ACTIVITY IDEAS

| VISUAL | AUDITORY |
|---|---|
| • | • |
| • | • |
| **FINE MOTOR** | **TACTILE** |
| • | • |
| • | • |

| # WEEK | | APPOINTMENTS | |
|---|---|---|---|
| 📅 DATE | | | : |
| 🕐 TIME | | | : |
| 📍 PLACE | | | : |

## 💬 COMMUNICATION GOALS

| ☐ | ☐ |
|---|---|
| ☐ | ☐ |
| ☐ | ☐ |

## 👥 SOCIAL SKILLS GOALS

| ☐ | ☐ |
|---|---|
| ☐ | ☐ |
| ☐ | ☐ |

## 🔺 SENSORY & O.T. GOALS

| ☐ | ☐ |
|---|---|
| ☐ | ☐ |
| ☐ | ☐ |

## 🧩 THERAPY ACTIVITY IDEAS

| VISUAL | AUDITORY |
|---|---|
| • | • |
| • | • |
| FINE MOTOR | TACTILE |
| • | • |
| • | • |

| # WEEK | APPOINTMENTS | |
|--------|--------------|---|
| ▦ DATE | | : |
| 🕐 TIME | | : |
| ◎ PLACE | | : |

## 💬 COMMUNICATION GOALS

| ☐ | ☐ |
|---|---|
| ☐ | ☐ |
| ☐ | ☐ |

## 👥 SOCIAL SKILLS GOALS

| ☐ | ☐ |
|---|---|
| ☐ | ☐ |
| ☐ | ☐ |

## SENSORY & O.T. GOALS

| ☐ | ☐ |
|---|---|
| ☐ | ☐ |
| ☐ | ☐ |

## 🧩 THERAPY ACTIVITY IDEAS

| VISUAL | AUDITORY |
|--------|----------|
| • | • |
| • | • |

| FINE MOTOR | TACTILE |
|------------|---------|
| • | • |
| • | • |

| # WEEK | APPOINTMENTS | |
|---|---|---|
| ▦ DATE | | : |
| 🕐 TIME | | : |
| 📍 PLACE | | : |

## 💬 COMMUNICATION GOALS

| ☐ | ☐ |
|---|---|
| ☐ | ☐ |
| ☐ | ☐ |

## 👥 SOCIAL SKILLS GOALS

| ☐ | ☐ |
|---|---|
| ☐ | ☐ |
| ☐ | ☐ |

## SENSORY & O.T. GOALS

| ☐ | ☐ |
|---|---|
| ☐ | ☐ |
| ☐ | ☐ |

## 🧩 THERAPY ACTIVITY IDEAS

| VISUAL | AUDITORY |
|---|---|
| • | • |
| • | • |
| **FINE MOTOR** | **TACTILE** |
| • | • |
| • | • |

| # WEEK | | APPOINTMENTS | |
|---|---|---|---|
| 📅 DATE | | | : |
| 🕐 TIME | | | : |
| 📍 PLACE | | | : |

## 💬 COMMUNICATION GOALS

| ☐ | ☐ |
|---|---|
| ☐ | ☐ |
| ☐ | ☐ |

## 👥 SOCIAL SKILLS GOALS

| ☐ | ☐ |
|---|---|
| ☐ | ☐ |
| ☐ | ☐ |

## SENSORY & O.T. GOALS

| ☐ | ☐ |
|---|---|
| ☐ | ☐ |
| ☐ | ☐ |

## 🧩 THERAPY ACTIVITY IDEAS

| VISUAL | AUDITORY |
|---|---|
| • | • |
| • | • |

| FINE MOTOR | TACTILE |
|---|---|
| • | • |
| • | • |

| # WEEK | | APPOINTMENTS | |
|---|---|---|---|
| 📅 DATE | | | : |
| 🕐 TIME | | | : |
| 📍 PLACE | | | : |

## 💬 COMMUNICATION GOALS

| ☐ | ☐ |
|---|---|
| ☐ | ☐ |
| ☐ | ☐ |

## 👥 SOCIAL SKILLS GOALS

| ☐ | ☐ |
|---|---|
| ☐ | ☐ |
| ☐ | ☐ |

## SENSORY & O.T. GOALS

| ☐ | ☐ |
|---|---|
| ☐ | ☐ |
| ☐ | ☐ |

## 🧩 THERAPY ACTIVITY IDEAS

| VISUAL | AUDITORY |
|---|---|
| • | • |
| • | • |

| FINE MOTOR | TACTILE |
|---|---|
| • | • |
| • | • |

| # WEEK | | APPOINTMENTS | |
|---|---|---|---|
| 📅 DATE | | | : |
| 🕐 TIME | | | : |
| 📍 PLACE | | | : |

## 💬 COMMUNICATION GOALS

| | |
|---|---|
| ☐ | ☐ |
| ☐ | ☐ |
| ☐ | ☐ |

## SOCIAL SKILLS GOALS

| | |
|---|---|
| ☐ | ☐ |
| ☐ | ☐ |
| ☐ | ☐ |

## SENSORY & O.T. GOALS

| | |
|---|---|
| ☐ | ☐ |
| ☐ | ☐ |
| ☐ | ☐ |

## 🧩 THERAPY ACTIVITY IDEAS

| VISUAL | AUDITORY |
|---|---|
| • | • |
| • | • |

| FINE MOTOR | TACTILE |
|---|---|
| • | • |
| • | • |

| # WEEK | | APPOINTMENTS | |
|---|---|---|---|
| 📅 DATE | | | : |
| 🕐 TIME | | | : |
| 📍 PLACE | | | : |

## 💬 COMMUNICATION GOALS

| ☐ | ☐ |
|---|---|
| ☐ | ☐ |
| ☐ | ☐ |

## 👥 SOCIAL SKILLS GOALS

| ☐ | ☐ |
|---|---|
| ☐ | ☐ |
| ☐ | ☐ |

## 🔺 SENSORY & O.T. GOALS

| ☐ | ☐ |
|---|---|
| ☐ | ☐ |
| ☐ | ☐ |

## 🧩 THERAPY ACTIVITY IDEAS

| VISUAL | AUDITORY |
|---|---|
| • | • |
| • | • |
| FINE MOTOR | TACTILE |
| • | • |
| • | • |

| # WEEK | | APPOINTMENTS | |
|---|---|---|---|
| 🗓 DATE | | | : |
| 🕐 TIME | | | : |
| 📍 PLACE | | | : |

## 💬 COMMUNICATION GOALS

| | | | |
|---|---|---|---|
| ☐ | | ☐ | |
| ☐ | | ☐ | |
| ☐ | | ☐ | |

## 👥 SOCIAL SKILLS GOALS

| | | | |
|---|---|---|---|
| ☐ | | ☐ | |
| ☐ | | ☐ | |
| ☐ | | ☐ | |

## 🔷 SENSORY & O.T. GOALS

| | | | |
|---|---|---|---|
| ☐ | | ☐ | |
| ☐ | | ☐ | |
| ☐ | | ☐ | |

## 🧩 THERAPY ACTIVITY IDEAS

| VISUAL | AUDITORY |
|---|---|
| • | • |
| • | • |

| FINE MOTOR | TACTILE |
|---|---|
| • | • |
| • | • |

| # WEEK | | APPOINTMENTS | |
|---|---|---|---|
| ▦ DATE | | | : |
| 🕐 TIME | | | : |
| 📍 PLACE | | | : |

## 💬 COMMUNICATION GOALS

| ☐ | ☐ |
|---|---|
| ☐ | ☐ |
| ☐ | ☐ |

## 👥 SOCIAL SKILLS GOALS

| ☐ | ☐ |
|---|---|
| ☐ | ☐ |
| ☐ | ☐ |

## SENSORY & O.T. GOALS

| ☐ | ☐ |
|---|---|
| ☐ | ☐ |
| ☐ | ☐ |

## 🧩 THERAPY ACTIVITY IDEAS

| VISUAL | AUDITORY |
|---|---|
| • | • |
| • | • |

| FINE MOTOR | TACTILE |
|---|---|
| • | • |
| • | • |

| # WEEK | | APPOINTMENTS | |
|---|---|---|---|
| 📅 DATE | | | : |
| 🕐 TIME | | | : |
| 📍 PLACE | | | : |

## 💬 COMMUNICATION GOALS

| ☐ | ☐ |
|---|---|
| ☐ | ☐ |
| ☐ | ☐ |

## 👥 SOCIAL SKILLS GOALS

| ☐ | ☐ |
|---|---|
| ☐ | ☐ |
| ☐ | ☐ |

## 🔀 SENSORY & O.T. GOALS

| ☐ | ☐ |
|---|---|
| ☐ | ☐ |
| ☐ | ☐ |

## 🧩 THERAPY ACTIVITY IDEAS

| VISUAL | AUDITORY |
|---|---|
| • | • |
| • | • |

| FINE MOTOR | TACTILE |
|---|---|
| • | • |
| • | • |

| # WEEK | APPOINTMENTS | |
|---|---|---|
| ▦ DATE | | : |
| ⏲ TIME | | : |
| ⊙ PLACE | | : |

## 💬 COMMUNICATION GOALS

| ☐ | ☐ |
|---|---|
| ☐ | ☐ |
| ☐ | ☐ |

## 🫂 SOCIAL SKILLS GOALS

| ☐ | ☐ |
|---|---|
| ☐ | ☐ |
| ☐ | ☐ |

## 🔷 SENSORY & O.T. GOALS

| ☐ | ☐ |
|---|---|
| ☐ | ☐ |
| ☐ | ☐ |

## 🧩 THERAPY ACTIVITY IDEAS

| VISUAL | AUDITORY |
|---|---|
| • | • |
| • | • |

| FINE MOTOR | TACTILE |
|---|---|
| • | • |
| • | • |

| # WEEK | | APPOINTMENTS | |
|---|---|---|---|
| ▦ DATE | | | : |
| 🕐 TIME | | | : |
| 🗺 PLACE | | | : |

## 💬 COMMUNICATION GOALS

| ☐ | ☐ |
|---|---|
| ☐ | ☐ |
| ☐ | ☐ |

## 👥 SOCIAL SKILLS GOALS

| ☐ | ☐ |
|---|---|
| ☐ | ☐ |
| ☐ | ☐ |

## 🔷 SENSORY & O.T. GOALS

| ☐ | ☐ |
|---|---|
| ☐ | ☐ |
| ☐ | ☐ |

## 🧩 THERAPY ACTIVITY IDEAS

| VISUAL | AUDITORY |
|---|---|
| • | • |
| • | • |

| FINE MOTOR | TACTILE |
|---|---|
| • | • |
| • | • |

| # WEEK | | APPOINTMENTS | |
|---|---|---|---|
| ▦ DATE | | | : |
| 🕐 TIME | | | : |
| 📍 PLACE | | | : |

## 💬 COMMUNICATION GOALS

| ☐ | ☐ |
|---|---|
| ☐ | ☐ |
| ☐ | ☐ |

## 👥 SOCIAL SKILLS GOALS

| ☐ | ☐ |
|---|---|
| ☐ | ☐ |
| ☐ | ☐ |

## SENSORY & O.T. GOALS

| ☐ | ☐ |
|---|---|
| ☐ | ☐ |
| ☐ | ☐ |

## 🧩 THERAPY ACTIVITY IDEAS

| VISUAL | AUDITORY |
|---|---|
| • | • |
| • | • |
| **FINE MOTOR** | **TACTILE** |
| • | • |
| • | • |

| # WEEK | | APPOINTMENTS | |
|---|---|---|---|
| ▦ DATE | | | : |
| ⏲ TIME | | | : |
| ⚲ PLACE | | | : |

## 💬 COMMUNICATION GOALS

| ☐ | ☐ |
|---|---|
| ☐ | ☐ |
| ☐ | ☐ |

## ⚇ SOCIAL SKILLS GOALS

| ☐ | ☐ |
|---|---|
| ☐ | ☐ |
| ☐ | ☐ |

## ◈ SENSORY & O.T. GOALS

| ☐ | ☐ |
|---|---|
| ☐ | ☐ |
| ☐ | ☐ |

## ⟐ THERAPY ACTIVITY IDEAS

| VISUAL | AUDITORY |
|---|---|
| • | • |
| • | • |
| **FINE MOTOR** | **TACTILE** |
| • | • |
| • | • |

| # WEEK | | APPOINTMENTS | |
|---|---|---|---|
| 📅 DATE | | | : |
| 🕐 TIME | | | : |
| 📍 PLACE | | | : |

## 💬 COMMUNICATION GOALS

| ☐ | ☐ |
|---|---|
| ☐ | ☐ |
| ☐ | ☐ |

## 👥 SOCIAL SKILLS GOALS

| ☐ | ☐ |
|---|---|
| ☐ | ☐ |
| ☐ | ☐ |

## 🔷 SENSORY & O.T. GOALS

| ☐ | ☐ |
|---|---|
| ☐ | ☐ |
| ☐ | ☐ |

## 🧩 THERAPY ACTIVITY IDEAS

| VISUAL | AUDITORY |
|---|---|
| • | • |
| • | • |
| **FINE MOTOR** | **TACTILE** |
| • | • |
| • | • |

| # WEEK | | APPOINTMENTS | |
|---|---|---|---|
| 📅 DATE | | | : |
| 🕐 TIME | | | : |
| 📍 PLACE | | | : |

## 💬 COMMUNICATION GOALS

| ☐ | ☐ |
|---|---|
| ☐ | ☐ |
| ☐ | ☐ |

## 👥 SOCIAL SKILLS GOALS

| ☐ | ☐ |
|---|---|
| ☐ | ☐ |
| ☐ | ☐ |

## 🔷 SENSORY & O.T. GOALS

| ☐ | ☐ |
|---|---|
| ☐ | ☐ |
| ☐ | ☐ |

## 🧩 THERAPY ACTIVITY IDEAS

| VISUAL | AUDITORY |
|---|---|
| • | • |
| • | • |

| FINE MOTOR | TACTILE |
|---|---|
| • | • |
| • | • |

| # WEEK | | APPOINTMENTS | |
|---|---|---|---|
| ▦ DATE | | | : |
| 🕐 TIME | | | : |
| ⊗ PLACE | | | : |

## 💬 COMMUNICATION GOALS

| ☐ | ☐ |
|---|---|
| ☐ | ☐ |
| ☐ | ☐ |

## 👥 SOCIAL SKILLS GOALS

| ☐ | ☐ |
|---|---|
| ☐ | ☐ |
| ☐ | ☐ |

## SENSORY & O.T. GOALS

| ☐ | ☐ |
|---|---|
| ☐ | ☐ |
| ☐ | ☐ |

## 🧩 THERAPY ACTIVITY IDEAS

| VISUAL | AUDITORY |
|---|---|
| • | • |
| • | • |
| FINE MOTOR | TACTILE |
| • | • |
| • | • |

| # WEEK | | APPOINTMENTS | |
|---|---|---|---|
| ▦ DATE | | | : |
| 🕐 TIME | | | : |
| ⊙ PLACE | | | : |

## 💬 COMMUNICATION GOALS

| ☐ | ☐ |
|---|---|
| ☐ | ☐ |
| ☐ | ☐ |

## 👥 SOCIAL SKILLS GOALS

| ☐ | ☐ |
|---|---|
| ☐ | ☐ |
| ☐ | ☐ |

## 🔲 SENSORY & O.T. GOALS

| ☐ | ☐ |
|---|---|
| ☐ | ☐ |
| ☐ | ☐ |

## 🧩 THERAPY ACTIVITY IDEAS

| VISUAL | AUDITORY |
|---|---|
| • | • |
| • | • |

| FINE MOTOR | TACTILE |
|---|---|
| • | • |
| • | • |

| # WEEK | | APPOINTMENTS | |
|---|---|---|---|
| ▦ DATE | | | : |
| 🕐 TIME | | | : |
| 📍 PLACE | | | : |

## 💬 COMMUNICATION GOALS

| ☐ | ☐ |
|---|---|
| ☐ | ☐ |
| ☐ | ☐ |

## 👥 SOCIAL SKILLS GOALS

| ☐ | ☐ |
|---|---|
| ☐ | ☐ |
| ☐ | ☐ |

## 🔷 SENSORY & O.T. GOALS

| ☐ | ☐ |
|---|---|
| ☐ | ☐ |
| ☐ | ☐ |

## 🧩 THERAPY ACTIVITY IDEAS

| VISUAL | AUDITORY |
|---|---|
| • | • |
| • | • |

| FINE MOTOR | TACTILE |
|---|---|
| • | • |
| • | • |

| # WEEK | | APPOINTMENTS | |
|---|---|---|---|
| 📅 DATE | | | : |
| 🕐 TIME | | | : |
| 📍 PLACE | | | : |

## 💬 COMMUNICATION GOALS

| ☐ | ☐ |
|---|---|
| ☐ | ☐ |
| ☐ | ☐ |

## 👥 SOCIAL SKILLS GOALS

| ☐ | ☐ |
|---|---|
| ☐ | ☐ |
| ☐ | ☐ |

## 🔷 SENSORY & O.T. GOALS

| ☐ | ☐ |
|---|---|
| ☐ | ☐ |
| ☐ | ☐ |

## 🧩 THERAPY ACTIVITY IDEAS

| VISUAL | AUDITORY |
|---|---|
| • | • |
| • | • |

| FINE MOTOR | TACTILE |
|---|---|
| • | • |
| • | • |

| # WEEK | APPOINTMENTS | |
|---|---|---|
| ▦ DATE | | : |
| 🕐 TIME | | : |
| ◎ PLACE | | : |

## 💬 COMMUNICATION GOALS

| ☐ | ☐ |
|---|---|
| ☐ | ☐ |
| ☐ | ☐ |

## 🔗 SOCIAL SKILLS GOALS

| ☐ | ☐ |
|---|---|
| ☐ | ☐ |
| ☐ | ☐ |

## SENSORY & O.T. GOALS

| ☐ | ☐ |
|---|---|
| ☐ | ☐ |
| ☐ | ☐ |

## 🧩 THERAPY ACTIVITY IDEAS

| VISUAL | AUDITORY |
|---|---|
| • | • |
| • | • |
| FINE MOTOR | TACTILE |
| • | • |
| • | • |

| # WEEK | | APPOINTMENTS | |
|---|---|---|---|
| 📅 DATE | | | : |
| 🕐 TIME | | | : |
| 📍 PLACE | | | : |

## 💬 COMMUNICATION GOALS

| ☐ | ☐ |
|---|---|
| ☐ | ☐ |
| ☐ | ☐ |

## 👥 SOCIAL SKILLS GOALS

| ☐ | ☐ |
|---|---|
| ☐ | ☐ |
| ☐ | ☐ |

## 🔺 SENSORY & O.T. GOALS

| ☐ | ☐ |
|---|---|
| ☐ | ☐ |
| ☐ | ☐ |

## 🧩 THERAPY ACTIVITY IDEAS

| VISUAL | AUDITORY |
|---|---|
| • | • |
| • | • |

| FINE MOTOR | TACTILE |
|---|---|
| • | • |
| • | • |

| # WEEK | | APPOINTMENTS | |
|---|---|---|---|
| 🗓 DATE | | | : |
| 🕐 TIME | | | : |
| 📍 PLACE | | | : |

## 💬 COMMUNICATION GOALS

| ☐ | ☐ |
|---|---|
| ☐ | ☐ |
| ☐ | ☐ |

## 👥 SOCIAL SKILLS GOALS

| ☐ | ☐ |
|---|---|
| ☐ | ☐ |
| ☐ | ☐ |

## 🔲 SENSORY & O.T. GOALS

| ☐ | ☐ |
|---|---|
| ☐ | ☐ |
| ☐ | ☐ |

## 🧩 THERAPY ACTIVITY IDEAS

| VISUAL | AUDITORY |
|---|---|
| • | • |
| • | • |
| **FINE MOTOR** | **TACTILE** |
| • | • |
| • | • |

| # WEEK | APPOINTMENTS | |
|---|---|---|
| 📅 DATE | | : |
| 🕐 TIME | | : |
| 📍 PLACE | | : |

## 💬 COMMUNICATION GOALS

| ☐ | ☐ |
|---|---|
| ☐ | ☐ |
| ☐ | ☐ |

## 👥 SOCIAL SKILLS GOALS

| ☐ | ☐ |
|---|---|
| ☐ | ☐ |
| ☐ | ☐ |

## 🔷 SENSORY & O.T. GOALS

| ☐ | ☐ |
|---|---|
| ☐ | ☐ |
| ☐ | ☐ |

## 🧩 THERAPY ACTIVITY IDEAS

| VISUAL | AUDITORY |
|---|---|
| • | • |
| • | • |

| FINE MOTOR | TACTILE |
|---|---|
| • | • |
| • | • |

| # WEEK | |
|---|---|
| ▦ DATE | |
| ⏱ TIME | |
| ⊚ PLACE | |

| APPOINTMENTS | |
|---|---|
| | : |
| | : |
| | : |

## 💬 COMMUNICATION GOALS

| ☐ | ☐ |
|---|---|
| ☐ | ☐ |
| ☐ | ☐ |

## 🎲 SOCIAL SKILLS GOALS

| ☐ | ☐ |
|---|---|
| ☐ | ☐ |
| ☐ | ☐ |

## SENSORY & O.T. GOALS

| ☐ | ☐ |
|---|---|
| ☐ | ☐ |
| ☐ | ☐ |

## 🧩 THERAPY ACTIVITY IDEAS

| VISUAL | AUDITORY |
|---|---|
| • | • |
| • | • |

| FINE MOTOR | TACTILE |
|---|---|
| • | • |
| • | • |

| # WEEK | | APPOINTMENTS | |
|---|---|---|---|
| 📅 DATE | | | : |
| 🕐 TIME | | | : |
| 📍 PLACE | | | : |

## 💬 COMMUNICATION GOALS

| | | | |
|---|---|---|---|
| ☐ | | ☐ | |
| ☐ | | ☐ | |
| ☐ | | ☐ | |

## 👥 SOCIAL SKILLS GOALS

| | | | |
|---|---|---|---|
| ☐ | | ☐ | |
| ☐ | | ☐ | |
| ☐ | | ☐ | |

## SENSORY & O.T. GOALS

| | | | |
|---|---|---|---|
| ☐ | | ☐ | |
| ☐ | | ☐ | |
| ☐ | | ☐ | |

## 🧩 THERAPY ACTIVITY IDEAS

| VISUAL | AUDITORY |
|---|---|
| • | • |
| • | • |

| FINE MOTOR | TACTILE |
|---|---|
| • | • |
| • | • |

| # WEEK | | APPOINTMENTS | |
|---|---|---|---|
| ▦ DATE | | | : |
| ⏱ TIME | | | : |
| ⊚ PLACE | | | : |

## 💬 COMMUNICATION GOALS

| ☐ | ☐ |
|---|---|
| ☐ | ☐ |
| ☐ | ☐ |

## ⊞ SOCIAL SKILLS GOALS

| ☐ | ☐ |
|---|---|
| ☐ | ☐ |
| ☐ | ☐ |

## ⬚ SENSORY & O.T. GOALS

| ☐ | ☐ |
|---|---|
| ☐ | ☐ |
| ☐ | ☐ |

## 🧩 THERAPY ACTIVITY IDEAS

| VISUAL | AUDITORY |
|---|---|
| • | • |
| • | • |

| FINE MOTOR | TACTILE |
|---|---|
| • | • |
| • | • |

| # WEEK | | APPOINTMENTS | |
|---|---|---|---|
| 🗓 DATE | | | : |
| 🕐 TIME | | | : |
| 📍 PLACE | | | : |

## 💬 COMMUNICATION GOALS

| ☐ | ☐ |
|---|---|
| ☐ | ☐ |
| ☐ | ☐ |

## 👥 SOCIAL SKILLS GOALS

| ☐ | ☐ |
|---|---|
| ☐ | ☐ |
| ☐ | ☐ |

## 🔲 SENSORY & O.T. GOALS

| ☐ | ☐ |
|---|---|
| ☐ | ☐ |
| ☐ | ☐ |

## 🧩 THERAPY ACTIVITY IDEAS

| VISUAL | AUDITORY |
|---|---|
| • | • |
| • | • |
| FINE MOTOR | TACTILE |
| • | • |
| • | • |

| # WEEK | | APPOINTMENTS | |
|---|---|---|---|
| 📅 DATE | | | : |
| 🕐 TIME | | | : |
| 📍 PLACE | | | : |

## 💬 COMMUNICATION GOALS

| ☐ | ☐ |
|---|---|
| ☐ | ☐ |
| ☐ | ☐ |

## 👥 SOCIAL SKILLS GOALS

| ☐ | ☐ |
|---|---|
| ☐ | ☐ |
| ☐ | ☐ |

## 🔷 SENSORY & O.T. GOALS

| ☐ | ☐ |
|---|---|
| ☐ | ☐ |
| ☐ | ☐ |

## 🧩 THERAPY ACTIVITY IDEAS

| VISUAL | AUDITORY |
|---|---|
| • | • |
| • | • |

| FINE MOTOR | TACTILE |
|---|---|
| • | • |
| • | • |

| # WEEK | | APPOINTMENTS | |
|---|---|---|---|
| 🗓 DATE | | | : |
| 🕐 TIME | | | : |
| 📍 PLACE | | | : |

## 💬 COMMUNICATION GOALS

| ☐ | ☐ |
|---|---|
| ☐ | ☐ |
| ☐ | ☐ |

## 👥 SOCIAL SKILLS GOALS

| ☐ | ☐ |
|---|---|
| ☐ | ☐ |
| ☐ | ☐ |

## 🔲 SENSORY & O.T. GOALS

| ☐ | ☐ |
|---|---|
| ☐ | ☐ |
| ☐ | ☐ |

## 🧩 THERAPY ACTIVITY IDEAS

| VISUAL | AUDITORY |
|---|---|
| • | • |
| • | • |
| FINE MOTOR | TACTILE |
| • | • |
| • | • |

| # WEEK | | APPOINTMENTS | |
|---|---|---|---|
| 🗓 DATE | | | : |
| 🕐 TIME | | | : |
| 📍 PLACE | | | : |

## 💬 COMMUNICATION GOALS

| ☐ | ☐ |
|---|---|
| ☐ | ☐ |
| ☐ | ☐ |

## 👥 SOCIAL SKILLS GOALS

| ☐ | ☐ |
|---|---|
| ☐ | ☐ |
| ☐ | ☐ |

## SENSORY & O.T. GOALS

| ☐ | ☐ |
|---|---|
| ☐ | ☐ |
| ☐ | ☐ |

## 🧩 THERAPY ACTIVITY IDEAS

| VISUAL | AUDITORY |
|---|---|
| • | • |
| • | • |

| FINE MOTOR | TACTILE |
|---|---|
| • | • |
| • | • |

| # WEEK | | APPOINTMENTS | |
|---|---|---|---|
| 📅 DATE | | | : |
| 🕐 TIME | | | : |
| 📍 PLACE | | | : |

## 💬 COMMUNICATION GOALS

| ☐ | ☐ |
|---|---|
| ☐ | ☐ |
| ☐ | ☐ |

## 👥 SOCIAL SKILLS GOALS

| ☐ | ☐ |
|---|---|
| ☐ | ☐ |
| ☐ | ☐ |

## 🔷 SENSORY & O.T. GOALS

| ☐ | ☐ |
|---|---|
| ☐ | ☐ |
| ☐ | ☐ |

## 🧩 THERAPY ACTIVITY IDEAS

| VISUAL | AUDITORY |
|---|---|
| • | • |
| • | • |
| **FINE MOTOR** | **TACTILE** |
| • | • |
| • | • |

| # WEEK | | APPOINTMENTS | |
|---|---|---|---|
| 📅 DATE | | | : |
| 🕐 TIME | | | : |
| 📍 PLACE | | | : |

### 💬 COMMUNICATION GOALS

| | |
|---|---|
| ☐ | ☐ |
| ☐ | ☐ |
| ☐ | ☐ |

### 👥 SOCIAL SKILLS GOALS

| | |
|---|---|
| ☐ | ☐ |
| ☐ | ☐ |
| ☐ | ☐ |

### 🧩 SENSORY & O.T. GOALS

| | |
|---|---|
| ☐ | ☐ |
| ☐ | ☐ |
| ☐ | ☐ |

### 🧩 THERAPY ACTIVITY IDEAS

| VISUAL | AUDITORY |
|---|---|
| • | • |
| • | • |

| FINE MOTOR | TACTILE |
|---|---|
| • | • |
| • | • |

| # WEEK | APPOINTMENTS | |
|---|---|---|
| 📅 DATE | | : |
| 🕐 TIME | | : |
| 📍 PLACE | | : |

### 💬 COMMUNICATION GOALS

| ☐ | ☐ |
|---|---|
| ☐ | ☐ |
| ☐ | ☐ |

### 👥 SOCIAL SKILLS GOALS

| ☐ | ☐ |
|---|---|
| ☐ | ☐ |
| ☐ | ☐ |

### 🧩 SENSORY & O.T. GOALS

| ☐ | ☐ |
|---|---|
| ☐ | ☐ |
| ☐ | ☐ |

### 🧩 THERAPY ACTIVITY IDEAS

| VISUAL | AUDITORY |
|---|---|
| • | • |
| • | • |

| FINE MOTOR | TACTILE |
|---|---|
| • | • |
| • | • |

| # WEEK | | APPOINTMENTS | |
|---|---|---|---|
| ▦ DATE | | | : |
| ⏲ TIME | | | : |
| ⊚ PLACE | | | : |

## 💬 COMMUNICATION GOALS

| ☐ | ☐ |
|---|---|
| ☐ | ☐ |
| ☐ | ☐ |

## 👥 SOCIAL SKILLS GOALS

| ☐ | ☐ |
|---|---|
| ☐ | ☐ |
| ☐ | ☐ |

## 🔶 SENSORY & O.T. GOALS

| ☐ | ☐ |
|---|---|
| ☐ | ☐ |
| ☐ | ☐ |

## 🧩 THERAPY ACTIVITY IDEAS

| VISUAL | AUDITORY |
|---|---|
| • | • |
| • | • |
| FINE MOTOR | TACTILE |
| • | • |
| • | • |

| # WEEK | APPOINTMENTS | |
|---|---|---|
| 🗓 DATE | | : |
| 🕐 TIME | | : |
| 📍 PLACE | | : |

## 💬 COMMUNICATION GOALS

| ☐ | ☐ |
|---|---|
| ☐ | ☐ |
| ☐ | ☐ |

## 👥 SOCIAL SKILLS GOALS

| ☐ | ☐ |
|---|---|
| ☐ | ☐ |
| ☐ | ☐ |

## 🔷 SENSORY & O.T. GOALS

| ☐ | ☐ |
|---|---|
| ☐ | ☐ |
| ☐ | ☐ |

## 🧩 THERAPY ACTIVITY IDEAS

| VISUAL | AUDITORY |
|---|---|
| • | • |
| • | • |

| FINE MOTOR | TACTILE |
|---|---|
| • | • |
| • | • |

| # WEEK | | APPOINTMENTS | |
|---|---|---|---|
| 📅 DATE | | | : |
| 🕐 TIME | | | : |
| 📍 PLACE | | | : |

## 💬 COMMUNICATION GOALS

| ☐ | ☐ |
|---|---|
| ☐ | ☐ |
| ☐ | ☐ |

## 👥 SOCIAL SKILLS GOALS

| ☐ | ☐ |
|---|---|
| ☐ | ☐ |
| ☐ | ☐ |

## 🔷 SENSORY & O.T. GOALS

| ☐ | ☐ |
|---|---|
| ☐ | ☐ |
| ☐ | ☐ |

## 🧩 THERAPY ACTIVITY IDEAS

| VISUAL | AUDITORY |
|---|---|
| • | • |
| • | • |
| FINE MOTOR | TACTILE |
| • | • |
| • | • |

| # WEEK | | APPOINTMENTS | |
|---|---|---|---|
| 📅 DATE | | | : |
| 🕐 TIME | | | : |
| 📍 PLACE | | | : |

## 💬 COMMUNICATION GOALS

| ☐ | ☐ |
|---|---|
| ☐ | ☐ |
| ☐ | ☐ |

## 👥 SOCIAL SKILLS GOALS

| ☐ | ☐ |
|---|---|
| ☐ | ☐ |
| ☐ | ☐ |

## 🔷 SENSORY & O.T. GOALS

| ☐ | ☐ |
|---|---|
| ☐ | ☐ |
| ☐ | ☐ |

## 🧩 THERAPY ACTIVITY IDEAS

| VISUAL | AUDITORY |
|---|---|
| • | • |
| • | • |

| FINE MOTOR | TACTILE |
|---|---|
| • | • |
| • | • |

| ![#] WEEK | | APPOINTMENTS | |
|---|---|---|---|
| ![📅] DATE | | | : |
| ![🕐] TIME | | | : |
| ![📍] PLACE | | | : |

## 💬 COMMUNICATION GOALS

| | |
|---|---|
| ☐ | ☐ |
| ☐ | ☐ |
| ☐ | ☐ |

## 👥 SOCIAL SKILLS GOALS

| | |
|---|---|
| ☐ | ☐ |
| ☐ | ☐ |
| ☐ | ☐ |

## SENSORY & O.T. GOALS

| | |
|---|---|
| ☐ | ☐ |
| ☐ | ☐ |
| ☐ | ☐ |

## 🧩 THERAPY ACTIVITY IDEAS

| VISUAL | AUDITORY |
|---|---|
| • | • |
| • | • |
| **FINE MOTOR** | **TACTILE** |
| • | • |
| • | • |

| # WEEK | | APPOINTMENTS | |
|---|---|---|---|
| 📅 DATE | | | : |
| 🕐 TIME | | | : |
| 📍 PLACE | | | : |

## 💬 COMMUNICATION GOALS

| ☐ | ☐ |
|---|---|
| ☐ | ☐ |
| ☐ | ☐ |

## 👥 SOCIAL SKILLS GOALS

| ☐ | ☐ |
|---|---|
| ☐ | ☐ |
| ☐ | ☐ |

## 🔷 SENSORY & O.T. GOALS

| ☐ | ☐ |
|---|---|
| ☐ | ☐ |
| ☐ | ☐ |

## 🧩 THERAPY ACTIVITY IDEAS

| VISUAL | AUDITORY |
|---|---|
| • | • |
| • | • |

| FINE MOTOR | TACTILE |
|---|---|
| • | • |
| • | • |

| # WEEK | APPOINTMENTS | |
|---|---|---|
| ▦ DATE | | : |
| 🕐 TIME | | : |
| 🗺 PLACE | | : |

## 💬 COMMUNICATION GOALS

| ☐ | ☐ |
|---|---|
| ☐ | ☐ |
| ☐ | ☐ |

## 👥 SOCIAL SKILLS GOALS

| ☐ | ☐ |
|---|---|
| ☐ | ☐ |
| ☐ | ☐ |

## SENSORY & O.T. GOALS

| ☐ | ☐ |
|---|---|
| ☐ | ☐ |
| ☐ | ☐ |

## 🧩 THERAPY ACTIVITY IDEAS

| VISUAL | AUDITORY |
|---|---|
| • | • |
| • | • |
| FINE MOTOR | TACTILE |
| • | • |
| • | • |

| [#] WEEK | APPOINTMENTS | |
|---|---|---|
| [📅] DATE | | : |
| [🕐] TIME | | : |
| [📍] PLACE | | : |

## 💬 COMMUNICATION GOALS

| ☐ | ☐ |
|---|---|
| ☐ | ☐ |
| ☐ | ☐ |

## 👥 SOCIAL SKILLS GOALS

| ☐ | ☐ |
|---|---|
| ☐ | ☐ |
| ☐ | ☐ |

## 🔷 SENSORY & O.T. GOALS

| ☐ | ☐ |
|---|---|
| ☐ | ☐ |
| ☐ | ☐ |

## 🧩 THERAPY ACTIVITY IDEAS

| VISUAL | AUDITORY |
|---|---|
| • | • |
| • | • |

| FINE MOTOR | TACTILE |
|---|---|
| • | • |
| • | • |

| # WEEK | | APPOINTMENTS | |
|---|---|---|---|
| 📅 DATE | | | : |
| 🕐 TIME | | | : |
| 📍 PLACE | | | : |

## 💬 COMMUNICATION GOALS

| ☐ | ☐ |
|---|---|
| ☐ | ☐ |
| ☐ | ☐ |

## 👥 SOCIAL SKILLS GOALS

| ☐ | ☐ |
|---|---|
| ☐ | ☐ |
| ☐ | ☐ |

## 🔲 SENSORY & O.T. GOALS

| ☐ | ☐ |
|---|---|
| ☐ | ☐ |
| ☐ | ☐ |

## 🧩 THERAPY ACTIVITY IDEAS

| VISUAL | AUDITORY |
|---|---|
| • | • |
| • | • |
| **FINE MOTOR** | **TACTILE** |
| • | • |
| • | • |

| | | APPOINTMENTS | |
|---|---|---|---|
| # WEEK | | | : |
| 📅 DATE | | | : |
| 🕐 TIME | | | : |
| 📍 PLACE | | | : |

## 💬 COMMUNICATION GOALS

| ☐ | ☐ |
|---|---|
| ☐ | ☐ |
| ☐ | ☐ |

## 👥 SOCIAL SKILLS GOALS

| ☐ | ☐ |
|---|---|
| ☐ | ☐ |
| ☐ | ☐ |

## 🔷 SENSORY & O.T. GOALS

| ☐ | ☐ |
|---|---|
| ☐ | ☐ |
| ☐ | ☐ |

## 🧩 THERAPY ACTIVITY IDEAS

| VISUAL | AUDITORY |
|---|---|
| • | • |
| • | • |
| **FINE MOTOR** | **TACTILE** |
| • | • |
| • | • |

| # WEEK | | APPOINTMENTS | |
|---|---|---|---|
| 📅 DATE | | | : |
| 🕐 TIME | | | : |
| 📍 PLACE | | | : |

## 💬 COMMUNICATION GOALS

| ☐ | ☐ |
|---|---|
| ☐ | ☐ |
| ☐ | ☐ |

## 👥 SOCIAL SKILLS GOALS

| ☐ | ☐ |
|---|---|
| ☐ | ☐ |
| ☐ | ☐ |

## SENSORY & O.T. GOALS

| ☐ | ☐ |
|---|---|
| ☐ | ☐ |
| ☐ | ☐ |

## 🧩 THERAPY ACTIVITY IDEAS

| VISUAL | AUDITORY |
|---|---|
| • | • |
| • | • |
| FINE MOTOR | TACTILE |
| • | • |
| • | • |

| # WEEK | | APPOINTMENTS | |
|---|---|---|---|
| 📅 DATE | | | : |
| 🕐 TIME | | | : |
| 📍 PLACE | | | : |

## 💬 COMMUNICATION GOALS

| ☐ | ☐ |
|---|---|
| ☐ | ☐ |
| ☐ | ☐ |

## 👥 SOCIAL SKILLS GOALS

| ☐ | ☐ |
|---|---|
| ☐ | ☐ |
| ☐ | ☐ |

## 🔲 SENSORY & O.T. GOALS

| ☐ | ☐ |
|---|---|
| ☐ | ☐ |
| ☐ | ☐ |

## 🧩 THERAPY ACTIVITY IDEAS

| VISUAL | AUDITORY |
|---|---|
| • | • |
| • | • |

| FINE MOTOR | TACTILE |
|---|---|
| • | • |
| • | • |

| # WEEK | | APPOINTMENTS | |
|---|---|---|---|
| 📅 DATE | | | : |
| 🕐 TIME | | | : |
| 📍 PLACE | | | : |

## 💬 COMMUNICATION GOALS

| ☐ | ☐ |
|---|---|
| ☐ | ☐ |
| ☐ | ☐ |

## 👥 SOCIAL SKILLS GOALS

| ☐ | ☐ |
|---|---|
| ☐ | ☐ |
| ☐ | ☐ |

## 🔲 SENSORY & O.T. GOALS

| ☐ | ☐ |
|---|---|
| ☐ | ☐ |
| ☐ | ☐ |

## 🧩 THERAPY ACTIVITY IDEAS

| VISUAL | AUDITORY |
|---|---|
| • | • |
| • | • |
| FINE MOTOR | TACTILE |
| • | • |
| • | • |

| # WEEK | | APPOINTMENTS | |
|---|---|---|---|
| 📅 DATE | | | : |
| 🕐 TIME | | | : |
| 📍 PLACE | | | : |

## 💬 COMMUNICATION GOALS

| ☐ | ☐ |
|---|---|
| ☐ | ☐ |
| ☐ | ☐ |

## 👥 SOCIAL SKILLS GOALS

| ☐ | ☐ |
|---|---|
| ☐ | ☐ |
| ☐ | ☐ |

## 🔷 SENSORY & O.T. GOALS

| ☐ | ☐ |
|---|---|
| ☐ | ☐ |
| ☐ | ☐ |

## 🧩 THERAPY ACTIVITY IDEAS

| VISUAL | AUDITORY |
|---|---|
| • | • |
| • | • |
| FINE MOTOR | TACTILE |
| • | • |
| • | • |

| # WEEK | | APPOINTMENTS | |
|---|---|---|---|
| 📅 DATE | | | : |
| 🕐 TIME | | | : |
| 📍 PLACE | | | : |

## 💬 COMMUNICATION GOALS

| | |
|---|---|
| ☐ | ☐ |
| ☐ | ☐ |
| ☐ | ☐ |

## 👥 SOCIAL SKILLS GOALS

| | |
|---|---|
| ☐ | ☐ |
| ☐ | ☐ |
| ☐ | ☐ |

## 🔷 SENSORY & O.T. GOALS

| | |
|---|---|
| ☐ | ☐ |
| ☐ | ☐ |
| ☐ | ☐ |

## 🧩 THERAPY ACTIVITY IDEAS

| VISUAL | AUDITORY |
|---|---|
| • | • |
| • | • |
| **FINE MOTOR** | **TACTILE** |
| • | • |
| • | • |

| # WEEK | | APPOINTMENTS | |
|---|---|---|---|
| ▦ DATE | | | : |
| ⏱ TIME | | | : |
| ⊙ PLACE | | | : |

## 💬 COMMUNICATION GOALS

| ☐ | ☐ |
|---|---|
| ☐ | ☐ |
| ☐ | ☐ |

## 👥 SOCIAL SKILLS GOALS

| ☐ | ☐ |
|---|---|
| ☐ | ☐ |
| ☐ | ☐ |

## SENSORY & O.T. GOALS

| ☐ | ☐ |
|---|---|
| ☐ | ☐ |
| ☐ | ☐ |

## 🧩 THERAPY ACTIVITY IDEAS

| VISUAL | AUDITORY |
|---|---|
| • | • |
| • | • |
| FINE MOTOR | TACTILE |
| • | • |
| • | • |

| # WEEK | APPOINTMENTS | |
|--------|--------------|---|
| 📅 DATE | | : |
| 🕐 TIME | | : |
| 📍 PLACE | | : |

## 💬 COMMUNICATION GOALS

| ☐ | ☐ |
|---|---|
| ☐ | ☐ |
| ☐ | ☐ |

## 👥 SOCIAL SKILLS GOALS

| ☐ | ☐ |
|---|---|
| ☐ | ☐ |
| ☐ | ☐ |

## SENSORY & O.T. GOALS

| ☐ | ☐ |
|---|---|
| ☐ | ☐ |
| ☐ | ☐ |

## 🧩 THERAPY ACTIVITY IDEAS

| VISUAL | AUDITORY |
|--------|----------|
| • | • |
| • | • |

| FINE MOTOR | TACTILE |
|------------|---------|
| • | • |
| • | • |

| # WEEK | APPOINTMENTS | |
|---|---|---|
| 📅 DATE | | : |
| 🕐 TIME | | : |
| 📍 PLACE | | : |

## 💬 COMMUNICATION GOALS

| ☐ | ☐ |
|---|---|
| ☐ | ☐ |
| ☐ | ☐ |

## 👥 SOCIAL SKILLS GOALS

| ☐ | ☐ |
|---|---|
| ☐ | ☐ |
| ☐ | ☐ |

## 🔺 SENSORY & O.T. GOALS

| ☐ | ☐ |
|---|---|
| ☐ | ☐ |
| ☐ | ☐ |

## 🧩 THERAPY ACTIVITY IDEAS

| VISUAL | AUDITORY |
|---|---|
| • | • |
| • | • |
| **FINE MOTOR** | **TACTILE** |
| • | • |
| • | • |

| # WEEK | | APPOINTMENTS | |
|---|---|---|---|
| 📅 DATE | | | : |
| 🕐 TIME | | | : |
| 📍 PLACE | | | : |

## 💬 COMMUNICATION GOALS

| ☐ | ☐ |
|---|---|
| ☐ | ☐ |
| ☐ | ☐ |

## 👥 SOCIAL SKILLS GOALS

| ☐ | ☐ |
|---|---|
| ☐ | ☐ |
| ☐ | ☐ |

## SENSORY & O.T. GOALS

| ☐ | ☐ |
|---|---|
| ☐ | ☐ |
| ☐ | ☐ |

## 🧩 THERAPY ACTIVITY IDEAS

| VISUAL | AUDITORY |
|---|---|
| • | • |
| • | • |

| FINE MOTOR | TACTILE |
|---|---|
| • | • |
| • | • |

| # WEEK | | APPOINTMENTS | |
|---|---|---|---|
| 📅 DATE | | | : |
| 🕐 TIME | | | : |
| 📍 PLACE | | | : |

## 💬 COMMUNICATION GOALS

| ☐ | ☐ |
|---|---|
| ☐ | ☐ |
| ☐ | ☐ |

## 👥 SOCIAL SKILLS GOALS

| ☐ | ☐ |
|---|---|
| ☐ | ☐ |
| ☐ | ☐ |

## 🧩 SENSORY & O.T. GOALS

| ☐ | ☐ |
|---|---|
| ☐ | ☐ |
| ☐ | ☐ |

## 🧩 THERAPY ACTIVITY IDEAS

| VISUAL | AUDITORY |
|---|---|
| • | • |
| • | • |
| FINE MOTOR | TACTILE |
| • | • |
| • | • |

| # WEEK | | APPOINTMENTS | |
|---|---|---|---|
| ▦ DATE | | | : |
| ⏱ TIME | | | : |
| ⌖ PLACE | | | : |

## 💬 COMMUNICATION GOALS

| ☐ | ☐ |
|---|---|
| ☐ | ☐ |
| ☐ | ☐ |

## 👥 SOCIAL SKILLS GOALS

| ☐ | ☐ |
|---|---|
| ☐ | ☐ |
| ☐ | ☐ |

## SENSORY & O.T. GOALS

| ☐ | ☐ |
|---|---|
| ☐ | ☐ |
| ☐ | ☐ |

## 🧩 THERAPY ACTIVITY IDEAS

| VISUAL | AUDITORY |
|---|---|
| • | • |
| • | • |

| FINE MOTOR | TACTILE |
|---|---|
| • | • |
| • | • |

| # WEEK | APPOINTMENTS | |
|---|---|---|
| 📅 DATE | | : |
| 🕐 TIME | | : |
| 📍 PLACE | | : |

## 💬 COMMUNICATION GOALS

| ☐ | ☐ |
|---|---|
| ☐ | ☐ |
| ☐ | ☐ |

## 👥 SOCIAL SKILLS GOALS

| ☐ | ☐ |
|---|---|
| ☐ | ☐ |
| ☐ | ☐ |

## 🔲 SENSORY & O.T. GOALS

| ☐ | ☐ |
|---|---|
| ☐ | ☐ |
| ☐ | ☐ |

## 🧩 THERAPY ACTIVITY IDEAS

| VISUAL | AUDITORY |
|---|---|
| • | • |
| • | • |
| FINE MOTOR | TACTILE |
| • | • |
| • | • |

| # WEEK | | APPOINTMENTS | |
|---|---|---|---|
| ⊞ DATE | | | : |
| ⧖ TIME | | | : |
| ⊗ PLACE | | | : |

## 💬 COMMUNICATION GOALS

| ☐ | ☐ |
|---|---|
| ☐ | ☐ |
| ☐ | ☐ |

## SOCIAL SKILLS GOALS

| ☐ | ☐ |
|---|---|
| ☐ | ☐ |
| ☐ | ☐ |

## SENSORY & O.T. GOALS

| ☐ | ☐ |
|---|---|
| ☐ | ☐ |
| ☐ | ☐ |

## 🧩 THERAPY ACTIVITY IDEAS

| VISUAL | AUDITORY |
|---|---|
| • | • |
| • | • |
| FINE MOTOR | TACTILE |
| • | • |
| • | • |

| # WEEK | APPOINTMENTS | |
|---|---|---|
| 🗓 DATE | | : |
| 🕐 TIME | | : |
| 📍 PLACE | | : |

## 💬 COMMUNICATION GOALS

| ☐ | ☐ |
|---|---|
| ☐ | ☐ |
| ☐ | ☐ |

## 👥 SOCIAL SKILLS GOALS

| ☐ | ☐ |
|---|---|
| ☐ | ☐ |
| ☐ | ☐ |

## 🔷 SENSORY & O.T. GOALS

| ☐ | ☐ |
|---|---|
| ☐ | ☐ |
| ☐ | ☐ |

## 🧩 THERAPY ACTIVITY IDEAS

| VISUAL | AUDITORY |
|---|---|
| • | • |
| • | • |

| FINE MOTOR | TACTILE |
|---|---|
| • | • |
| • | • |

| # WEEK | | APPOINTMENTS | |
|---|---|---|---|
| ▦ DATE | | | : |
| 🕐 TIME | | | : |
| 📍 PLACE | | | : |

## 💬 COMMUNICATION GOALS

| ☐ | ☐ |
|---|---|
| ☐ | ☐ |
| ☐ | ☐ |

## 👥 SOCIAL SKILLS GOALS

| ☐ | ☐ |
|---|---|
| ☐ | ☐ |
| ☐ | ☐ |

## 🔲 SENSORY & O.T. GOALS

| ☐ | ☐ |
|---|---|
| ☐ | ☐ |
| ☐ | ☐ |

## 🧩 THERAPY ACTIVITY IDEAS

| VISUAL | AUDITORY |
|---|---|
| • | • |
| • | • |

| FINE MOTOR | TACTILE |
|---|---|
| • | • |
| • | • |

| # WEEK | APPOINTMENTS | |
|---|---|---|
| 📅 DATE | | : |
| 🕐 TIME | | : |
| 📍 PLACE | | : |

## 💬 COMMUNICATION GOALS

| | |
|---|---|
| ☐ | ☐ |
| ☐ | ☐ |
| ☐ | ☐ |

## 👥 SOCIAL SKILLS GOALS

| | |
|---|---|
| ☐ | ☐ |
| ☐ | ☐ |
| ☐ | ☐ |

## 🔷 SENSORY & O.T. GOALS

| | |
|---|---|
| ☐ | ☐ |
| ☐ | ☐ |
| ☐ | ☐ |

## 🧩 THERAPY ACTIVITY IDEAS

| VISUAL | AUDITORY |
|---|---|
| • | • |
| • | • |
| **FINE MOTOR** | **TACTILE** |
| • | • |
| • | • |

| # WEEK | | APPOINTMENTS | |
|---|---|---|---|
| ▦ DATE | | | : |
| 🕐 TIME | | | : |
| 📍 PLACE | | | : |

## 💬 COMMUNICATION GOALS

| ☐ | ☐ |
|---|---|
| ☐ | ☐ |
| ☐ | ☐ |

## 👥 SOCIAL SKILLS GOALS

| ☐ | ☐ |
|---|---|
| ☐ | ☐ |
| ☐ | ☐ |

## 🔲 SENSORY & O.T. GOALS

| ☐ | ☐ |
|---|---|
| ☐ | ☐ |
| ☐ | ☐ |

## 🧩 THERAPY ACTIVITY IDEAS

| VISUAL | AUDITORY |
|---|---|
| • | • |
| • | • |

| FINE MOTOR | TACTILE |
|---|---|
| • | • |
| • | • |

| # WEEK | APPOINTMENTS | |
|---|---|---|
| 📅 DATE | | : |
| 🕐 TIME | | : |
| 📍 PLACE | | : |

## 💬 COMMUNICATION GOALS

| ☐ | ☐ |
|---|---|
| ☐ | ☐ |
| ☐ | ☐ |

## 👥 SOCIAL SKILLS GOALS

| ☐ | ☐ |
|---|---|
| ☐ | ☐ |
| ☐ | ☐ |

## 🔷 SENSORY & O.T. GOALS

| ☐ | ☐ |
|---|---|
| ☐ | ☐ |
| ☐ | ☐ |

## 🧩 THERAPY ACTIVITY IDEAS

| VISUAL | AUDITORY |
|---|---|
| • | • |
| • | • |

| FINE MOTOR | TACTILE |
|---|---|
| • | • |
| • | • |

| # WEEK | | APPOINTMENTS | |
|---|---|---|---|
| 📅 DATE | | | : |
| 🕐 TIME | | | : |
| 📍 PLACE | | | : |

## 💬 COMMUNICATION GOALS

| ☐ | ☐ |
|---|---|
| ☐ | ☐ |
| ☐ | ☐ |

## 👥 SOCIAL SKILLS GOALS

| ☐ | ☐ |
|---|---|
| ☐ | ☐ |
| ☐ | ☐ |

## SENSORY & O.T. GOALS

| ☐ | ☐ |
|---|---|
| ☐ | ☐ |
| ☐ | ☐ |

## 🧩 THERAPY ACTIVITY IDEAS

| VISUAL | AUDITORY |
|---|---|
| • | • |
| • | • |

| FINE MOTOR | TACTILE |
|---|---|
| • | • |
| • | • |

| # WEEK | | APPOINTMENTS | |
|---|---|---|---|
| 📅 DATE | | | : |
| 🕐 TIME | | | : |
| 📍 PLACE | | | : |

## 💬 COMMUNICATION GOALS

| ☐ | ☐ |
|---|---|
| ☐ | ☐ |
| ☐ | ☐ |

## 👥 SOCIAL SKILLS GOALS

| ☐ | ☐ |
|---|---|
| ☐ | ☐ |
| ☐ | ☐ |

## 🔷 SENSORY & O.T. GOALS

| ☐ | ☐ |
|---|---|
| ☐ | ☐ |
| ☐ | ☐ |

## 🧩 THERAPY ACTIVITY IDEAS

| VISUAL | AUDITORY |
|---|---|
| • | • |
| • | • |
| FINE MOTOR | TACTILE |
| • | • |
| • | • |

| # WEEK | APPOINTMENTS | |
|---|---|---|
| ▦ DATE | | : |
| 🕐 TIME | | : |
| ⊗ PLACE | | : |

## 💬 COMMUNICATION GOALS

| ☐ | ☐ |
|---|---|
| ☐ | ☐ |
| ☐ | ☐ |

## 👥 SOCIAL SKILLS GOALS

| ☐ | ☐ |
|---|---|
| ☐ | ☐ |
| ☐ | ☐ |

## SENSORY & O.T. GOALS

| ☐ | ☐ |
|---|---|
| ☐ | ☐ |
| ☐ | ☐ |

## 🧩 THERAPY ACTIVITY IDEAS

| VISUAL | AUDITORY |
|---|---|
| • | • |
| • | • |
| **FINE MOTOR** | **TACTILE** |
| • | • |
| • | • |

| # WEEK | APPOINTMENTS | |
|---|---|---|
| 📅 DATE | | : |
| 🕐 TIME | | : |
| 📍 PLACE | | : |

## 💬 COMMUNICATION GOALS

| ☐ | ☐ |
|---|---|
| ☐ | ☐ |
| ☐ | ☐ |

## 👥 SOCIAL SKILLS GOALS

| ☐ | ☐ |
|---|---|
| ☐ | ☐ |
| ☐ | ☐ |

## 🔺 SENSORY & O.T. GOALS

| ☐ | ☐ |
|---|---|
| ☐ | ☐ |
| ☐ | ☐ |

## 🧩 THERAPY ACTIVITY IDEAS

| VISUAL | AUDITORY |
|---|---|
| • | • |
| • | • |

| FINE MOTOR | TACTILE |
|---|---|
| • | • |
| • | • |

| # WEEK | | APPOINTMENTS | |
|---|---|---|---|
| DATE | | | : |
| TIME | | | : |
| PLACE | | | : |

## COMMUNICATION GOALS

| ☐ | ☐ |
|---|---|
| ☐ | ☐ |
| ☐ | ☐ |

## SOCIAL SKILLS GOALS

| ☐ | ☐ |
|---|---|
| ☐ | ☐ |
| ☐ | ☐ |

## SENSORY & O.T. GOALS

| ☐ | ☐ |
|---|---|
| ☐ | ☐ |
| ☐ | ☐ |

## THERAPY ACTIVITY IDEAS

| VISUAL | AUDITORY |
|---|---|
| • | • |
| • | • |
| FINE MOTOR | TACTILE |
| • | • |
| • | • |

| # WEEK | | APPOINTMENTS | |
|---|---|---|---|
| ▦ DATE | | | : |
| 🕐 TIME | | | : |
| 📍 PLACE | | | : |

## 💬 COMMUNICATION GOALS

| ☐ | ☐ |
|---|---|
| ☐ | ☐ |
| ☐ | ☐ |

## 👥 SOCIAL SKILLS GOALS

| ☐ | ☐ |
|---|---|
| ☐ | ☐ |
| ☐ | ☐ |

## 🧩 SENSORY & O.T. GOALS

| ☐ | ☐ |
|---|---|
| ☐ | ☐ |
| ☐ | ☐ |

## 🧩 THERAPY ACTIVITY IDEAS

| VISUAL | AUDITORY |
|---|---|
| • | • |
| • | • |

| FINE MOTOR | TACTILE |
|---|---|
| • | • |
| • | • |

| # WEEK | | APPOINTMENTS | |
|---|---|---|---|
| 📅 DATE | | | : |
| 🕐 TIME | | | : |
| 📍 PLACE | | | : |

## 💬 COMMUNICATION GOALS

| ☐ | ☐ |
|---|---|
| ☐ | ☐ |
| ☐ | ☐ |

## 👥 SOCIAL SKILLS GOALS

| ☐ | ☐ |
|---|---|
| ☐ | ☐ |
| ☐ | ☐ |

## 🧩 SENSORY & O.T. GOALS

| ☐ | ☐ |
|---|---|
| ☐ | ☐ |
| ☐ | ☐ |

## 🧩 THERAPY ACTIVITY IDEAS

| VISUAL | AUDITORY |
|---|---|
| • | • |
| • | • |

| FINE MOTOR | TACTILE |
|---|---|
| • | • |
| • | • |

| # WEEK | | APPOINTMENTS | |
|---|---|---|---|
| 📅 DATE | | | : |
| 🕐 TIME | | | : |
| 📍 PLACE | | | : |

## 💬 COMMUNICATION GOALS

| ☐ | ☐ |
|---|---|
| ☐ | ☐ |
| ☐ | ☐ |

## SOCIAL SKILLS GOALS

| ☐ | ☐ |
|---|---|
| ☐ | ☐ |
| ☐ | ☐ |

## SENSORY & O.T. GOALS

| ☐ | ☐ |
|---|---|
| ☐ | ☐ |
| ☐ | ☐ |

## 🧩 THERAPY ACTIVITY IDEAS

| VISUAL | AUDITORY |
|---|---|
| • | • |
| • | • |
| FINE MOTOR | TACTILE |
| • | • |
| • | • |

| # WEEK | | APPOINTMENTS | |
|---|---|---|---|
| ▦ DATE | | | : |
| 🕐 TIME | | | : |
| 📍 PLACE | | | : |

## 💬 COMMUNICATION GOALS

| ☐ | ☐ |
|---|---|
| ☐ | ☐ |
| ☐ | ☐ |

## 👥 SOCIAL SKILLS GOALS

| ☐ | ☐ |
|---|---|
| ☐ | ☐ |
| ☐ | ☐ |

## 🔲 SENSORY & O.T. GOALS

| ☐ | ☐ |
|---|---|
| ☐ | ☐ |
| ☐ | ☐ |

## 🧩 THERAPY ACTIVITY IDEAS

| VISUAL | AUDITORY |
|---|---|
| • | • |
| • | • |

| FINE MOTOR | TACTILE |
|---|---|
| • | • |
| • | • |

| # WEEK | | APPOINTMENTS | |
|---|---|---|---|
| DATE | | | : |
| TIME | | | : |
| PLACE | | | : |

## 💬 COMMUNICATION GOALS

| ☐ | ☐ |
|---|---|
| ☐ | ☐ |
| ☐ | ☐ |

## 👥 SOCIAL SKILLS GOALS

| ☐ | ☐ |
|---|---|
| ☐ | ☐ |
| ☐ | ☐ |

## SENSORY & O.T. GOALS

| ☐ | ☐ |
|---|---|
| ☐ | ☐ |
| ☐ | ☐ |

## 🧩 THERAPY ACTIVITY IDEAS

| VISUAL | AUDITORY |
|---|---|
| • | • |
| • | • |

| FINE MOTOR | TACTILE |
|---|---|
| • | • |
| • | • |

| # WEEK | | APPOINTMENTS | |
|---|---|---|---|
| ▦ DATE | | | : |
| 🕐 TIME | | | : |
| ◎ PLACE | | | : |

## 💬 COMMUNICATION GOALS

| ☐ | ☐ |
|---|---|
| ☐ | ☐ |
| ☐ | ☐ |

## 👥 SOCIAL SKILLS GOALS

| ☐ | ☐ |
|---|---|
| ☐ | ☐ |
| ☐ | ☐ |

## 🔷 SENSORY & O.T. GOALS

| ☐ | ☐ |
|---|---|
| ☐ | ☐ |
| ☐ | ☐ |

## 🧩 THERAPY ACTIVITY IDEAS

| VISUAL | AUDITORY |
|---|---|
| • | • |
| • | • |

| FINE MOTOR | TACTILE |
|---|---|
| • | • |
| • | • |

| # WEEK | | APPOINTMENTS | |
|---|---|---|---|
| 📅 DATE | | | : |
| 🕐 TIME | | | : |
| 📍 PLACE | | | : |

## 💬 COMMUNICATION GOALS

| ☐ | ☐ |
|---|---|
| ☐ | ☐ |
| ☐ | ☐ |

## 👥 SOCIAL SKILLS GOALS

| ☐ | ☐ |
|---|---|
| ☐ | ☐ |
| ☐ | ☐ |

## SENSORY & O.T. GOALS

| ☐ | ☐ |
|---|---|
| ☐ | ☐ |
| ☐ | ☐ |

## 🧩 THERAPY ACTIVITY IDEAS

| VISUAL | AUDITORY |
|---|---|
| • | • |
| • | • |

| FINE MOTOR | TACTILE |
|---|---|
| • | • |
| • | • |

| # WEEK | | APPOINTMENTS | |
|---|---|---|---|
| 📅 DATE | | | : |
| 🕐 TIME | | | : |
| 📍 PLACE | | | : |

## 💬 COMMUNICATION GOALS

| ☐ | ☐ |
|---|---|
| ☐ | ☐ |
| ☐ | ☐ |

## 👥 SOCIAL SKILLS GOALS

| ☐ | ☐ |
|---|---|
| ☐ | ☐ |
| ☐ | ☐ |

## SENSORY & O.T. GOALS

| ☐ | ☐ |
|---|---|
| ☐ | ☐ |
| ☐ | ☐ |

## 🧩 THERAPY ACTIVITY IDEAS

| VISUAL | AUDITORY |
|---|---|
| • | • |
| • | • |

| FINE MOTOR | TACTILE |
|---|---|
| • | • |
| • | • |

| # WEEK | | APPOINTMENTS | |
|---|---|---|---|
| 📅 DATE | | | : |
| 🕐 TIME | | | : |
| 📍 PLACE | | | : |

## 💬 COMMUNICATION GOALS

| ☐ | ☐ |
|---|---|
| ☐ | ☐ |
| ☐ | ☐ |

## 👥 SOCIAL SKILLS GOALS

| ☐ | ☐ |
|---|---|
| ☐ | ☐ |
| ☐ | ☐ |

## 🔷 SENSORY & O.T. GOALS

| ☐ | ☐ |
|---|---|
| ☐ | ☐ |
| ☐ | ☐ |

## 🧩 THERAPY ACTIVITY IDEAS

| VISUAL | AUDITORY |
|---|---|
| • | • |
| • | • |
| **FINE MOTOR** | **TACTILE** |
| • | • |
| • | • |

| # WEEK | | APPOINTMENTS | |
|---|---|---|---|
| 🗓 DATE | | | : |
| 🕐 TIME | | | : |
| 📍 PLACE | | | : |

## 💬 COMMUNICATION GOALS

| | |
|---|---|
| ☐ | ☐ |
| ☐ | ☐ |
| ☐ | ☐ |

## 👥 SOCIAL SKILLS GOALS

| | |
|---|---|
| ☐ | ☐ |
| ☐ | ☐ |
| ☐ | ☐ |

## 🔷 SENSORY & O.T. GOALS

| | |
|---|---|
| ☐ | ☐ |
| ☐ | ☐ |
| ☐ | ☐ |

## 🧩 THERAPY ACTIVITY IDEAS

| VISUAL | AUDITORY |
|---|---|
| • | • |
| • | • |

| FINE MOTOR | TACTILE |
|---|---|
| • | • |
| • | • |

| # WEEK | | APPOINTMENTS | |
|---|---|---|---|
| 📅 DATE | | | : |
| 🕐 TIME | | | : |
| 📍 PLACE | | | : |

## 💬 COMMUNICATION GOALS

| ☐ | ☐ |
|---|---|
| ☐ | ☐ |
| ☐ | ☐ |

## 👥 SOCIAL SKILLS GOALS

| ☐ | ☐ |
|---|---|
| ☐ | ☐ |
| ☐ | ☐ |

## 🔷 SENSORY & O.T. GOALS

| ☐ | ☐ |
|---|---|
| ☐ | ☐ |
| ☐ | ☐ |

## 🧩 THERAPY ACTIVITY IDEAS

| VISUAL | AUDITORY |
|---|---|
| • | • |
| • | • |

| FINE MOTOR | TACTILE |
|---|---|
| • | • |
| • | • |

| # WEEK | | APPOINTMENTS | |
|---|---|---|---|
| 📅 DATE | | | : |
| 🕐 TIME | | | : |
| 📍 PLACE | | | : |

## 💬 COMMUNICATION GOALS

| ☐ | ☐ |
|---|---|
| ☐ | ☐ |
| ☐ | ☐ |

## 👥 SOCIAL SKILLS GOALS

| ☐ | ☐ |
|---|---|
| ☐ | ☐ |
| ☐ | ☐ |

## SENSORY & O.T. GOALS

| ☐ | ☐ |
|---|---|
| ☐ | ☐ |
| ☐ | ☐ |

## 🧩 THERAPY ACTIVITY IDEAS

| VISUAL | AUDITORY |
|---|---|
| • | • |
| • | • |

| FINE MOTOR | TACTILE |
|---|---|
| • | • |
| • | • |

| # WEEK | APPOINTMENTS | |
|---|---|---|
| 📅 DATE | | : |
| 🕐 TIME | | : |
| 📍 PLACE | | : |

## 💬 COMMUNICATION GOALS

| | |
|---|---|
| ☐ | ☐ |
| ☐ | ☐ |
| ☐ | ☐ |

## 👥 SOCIAL SKILLS GOALS

| | |
|---|---|
| ☐ | ☐ |
| ☐ | ☐ |
| ☐ | ☐ |

## 🔷 SENSORY & O.T. GOALS

| | |
|---|---|
| ☐ | ☐ |
| ☐ | ☐ |
| ☐ | ☐ |

## 🧩 THERAPY ACTIVITY IDEAS

| VISUAL | AUDITORY |
|---|---|
| • | • |
| • | • |

| FINE MOTOR | TACTILE |
|---|---|
| • | • |
| • | • |

| # WEEK | | APPOINTMENTS | |
|---|---|---|---|
| ▦ DATE | | | : |
| ◷ TIME | | | : |
| ⊚ PLACE | | | : |

## 💬 COMMUNICATION GOALS

| ☐ | ☐ |
|---|---|
| ☐ | ☐ |
| ☐ | ☐ |

## SOCIAL SKILLS GOALS

| ☐ | ☐ |
|---|---|
| ☐ | ☐ |
| ☐ | ☐ |

## SENSORY & O.T. GOALS

| ☐ | ☐ |
|---|---|
| ☐ | ☐ |
| ☐ | ☐ |

## 🧩 THERAPY ACTIVITY IDEAS

| VISUAL | AUDITORY |
|---|---|
| • | • |
| • | • |

| FINE MOTOR | TACTILE |
|---|---|
| • | • |
| • | • |

| # WEEK | | APPOINTMENTS | |
| --- | --- | --- | --- |
| 📅 DATE | | | : |
| 🕐 TIME | | | : |
| 📍 PLACE | | | : |

## 💬 COMMUNICATION GOALS

| | | | |
| --- | --- | --- | --- |
| ☐ | | ☐ | |
| ☐ | | ☐ | |
| ☐ | | ☐ | |

## 👥 SOCIAL SKILLS GOALS

| | | | |
| --- | --- | --- | --- |
| ☐ | | ☐ | |
| ☐ | | ☐ | |
| ☐ | | ☐ | |

## SENSORY & O.T. GOALS

| | | | |
| --- | --- | --- | --- |
| ☐ | | ☐ | |
| ☐ | | ☐ | |
| ☐ | | ☐ | |

## 🧩 THERAPY ACTIVITY IDEAS

| VISUAL | AUDITORY |
| --- | --- |
| • | • |
| • | • |

| FINE MOTOR | TACTILE |
| --- | --- |
| • | • |
| • | • |

| # WEEK | APPOINTMENTS | |
|---|---|---|
| 🗓 DATE | | : |
| 🕐 TIME | | : |
| 📍 PLACE | | : |

## 💬 COMMUNICATION GOALS

| ☐ | ☐ |
|---|---|
| ☐ | ☐ |
| ☐ | ☐ |

## 👥 SOCIAL SKILLS GOALS

| ☐ | ☐ |
|---|---|
| ☐ | ☐ |
| ☐ | ☐ |

## 🔷 SENSORY & O.T. GOALS

| ☐ | ☐ |
|---|---|
| ☐ | ☐ |
| ☐ | ☐ |

## 🧩 THERAPY ACTIVITY IDEAS

| VISUAL | AUDITORY |
|---|---|
| • | • |
| • | • |

| FINE MOTOR | TACTILE |
|---|---|
| • | • |
| • | • |

| # WEEK | APPOINTMENTS | |
|---|---|---|
| 🗓 DATE | | : |
| 🕐 TIME | | : |
| 📍 PLACE | | : |

## 💬 COMMUNICATION GOALS

| ☐ | ☐ |
|---|---|
| ☐ | ☐ |
| ☐ | ☐ |

## 👥 SOCIAL SKILLS GOALS

| ☐ | ☐ |
|---|---|
| ☐ | ☐ |
| ☐ | ☐ |

## 🔷 SENSORY & O.T. GOALS

| ☐ | ☐ |
|---|---|
| ☐ | ☐ |
| ☐ | ☐ |

## 🧩 THERAPY ACTIVITY IDEAS

| VISUAL | AUDITORY |
|---|---|
| • | • |
| • | • |
| FINE MOTOR | TACTILE |
| • | • |
| • | • |

| # WEEK | | APPOINTMENTS | |
|---|---|---|---|
| ▦ DATE | | | : |
| 🕐 TIME | | | : |
| 📍 PLACE | | | : |

## 💬 COMMUNICATION GOALS

| ☐ | ☐ |
|---|---|
| ☐ | ☐ |
| ☐ | ☐ |

## 👥 SOCIAL SKILLS GOALS

| ☐ | ☐ |
|---|---|
| ☐ | ☐ |
| ☐ | ☐ |

## 🔣 SENSORY & O.T. GOALS

| ☐ | ☐ |
|---|---|
| ☐ | ☐ |
| ☐ | ☐ |

## 🧩 THERAPY ACTIVITY IDEAS

| VISUAL | AUDITORY |
|---|---|
| • | • |
| • | • |
| **FINE MOTOR** | **TACTILE** |
| • | • |
| • | • |

| # WEEK | | APPOINTMENTS | |
|---|---|---|---|
| 📅 DATE | | | : |
| 🕐 TIME | | | : |
| 📍 PLACE | | | : |

## 💬 COMMUNICATION GOALS

| ☐ | ☐ |
|---|---|
| ☐ | ☐ |
| ☐ | ☐ |

## 👥 SOCIAL SKILLS GOALS

| ☐ | ☐ |
|---|---|
| ☐ | ☐ |
| ☐ | ☐ |

## 🔲 SENSORY & O.T. GOALS

| ☐ | ☐ |
|---|---|
| ☐ | ☐ |
| ☐ | ☐ |

## 🧩 THERAPY ACTIVITY IDEAS

| VISUAL | AUDITORY |
|---|---|
| • | • |
| • | • |

| FINE MOTOR | TACTILE |
|---|---|
| • | • |
| • | • |

| # WEEK | APPOINTMENTS | |
|---|---|---|
| 📅 DATE | | : |
| 🕐 TIME | | : |
| 📍 PLACE | | : |

## 💬 COMMUNICATION GOALS

| ☐ | ☐ |
|---|---|
| ☐ | ☐ |
| ☐ | ☐ |

## 👥 SOCIAL SKILLS GOALS

| ☐ | ☐ |
|---|---|
| ☐ | ☐ |
| ☐ | ☐ |

## 🔶 SENSORY & O.T. GOALS

| ☐ | ☐ |
|---|---|
| ☐ | ☐ |
| ☐ | ☐ |

## 🧩 THERAPY ACTIVITY IDEAS

| VISUAL | AUDITORY |
|---|---|
| • | • |
| • | • |
| **FINE MOTOR** | **TACTILE** |
| • | • |
| • | • |

Made in United States
North Haven, CT
14 December 2024

62549647R00063